LOSE LESS

LAZY PUNTER REVEALS
HOW TO QUICKLY PICK MORE WINNING
HORSES WHILE STAYING MARRIED
AND KEEPING THE HOUSE!

JOHN CUTTS

1

Table of Contents

PREFACE

I have long felt the need to write this book.

I have not read a lot of books on horse racing betting but the ones I have left me no wiser after I read them.

They tend to be written (or ghost written) by ex-owners trainers or jockeys writing their memoirs, or pro gamblers with some stories but who give none of their 'secrets' away.

So, when the idea of finally (actually) writing a book came to me, I promised myself that the reader would finish the book having learned systems, methods, facts, that will help them in their future betting.

In fact, there are four or five "do this – do that – do this" systems in this book; the only logical guide to a 'value' price for a horse I have ever come across; and a guide to how to calculate the real (rather than the official) going, using race times.

As well as the *experts* keeping their *secrets* to themselves, another irritating thing has been the obvious padding of their books with irrelevant stories to make it look bigger and thus more 'valuable'.

Obviously, memoirs are stories and needn't offer any gambling advice.

But for me, a how-to, nonfiction book is worth what I learn from it and, though there are stories in my book, they are short and relevant to the discovery of this or that fact, system, method etc.

In short, I think there is a market for a book on horse racing betting that deals with topical debates like value vs winners, singles vs multiples, stake to size of bank ratios and more, but as the basis for immediately actionable advice rather than abstract nit picking.

Who am I to say? Well, I am no big shot pro gambler – that's for sure!

My first bet was on Red Rum in the 1973 Grand National, so you can tell how long I have been betting.

But I was only a kid back then and didn't begin betting seriously till the early nineties when my Brother and I were introduced to the system selections of someone who we still call the London Bloke to this day, even though we have known his name for decades.

We learned a lot in a short time back then and have been learning ever since as we continue the search for the London Bloke's system, which, for four and half years had an 80% strike rate at average odds against!

About a decade after his death, we had an inspiring winning run which we thought might enable us to quit the day job (glazing) and go pro. We also launched a new tipster service called Bet2Win.

We got rave reviews but, eventually, as with all systems, the bookies caught up with us. It still breaks even, and we still have some clients as subscribers for the selections even today – as part of other services in our portfolio.

So, since the 90's we have learned lots of lessons. There are nearly 30 years of experience, 30 years of trial and error and 30 years of joy and despair in the pages of this book.

For the past decade we have had a blog called thepunterspal.com and I have spent the past six months sifting through hundreds of our blog posts to select the very best – the most enlightening and those which underpin the systems and methods we reveal in the book.

Since then, I have carefully edited and fact checked them.

So, I have spent a good six months putting this book together and it will take you an hour or so to read it. No fluff. A how – to book that tells you precisely what to do, how to do it, and why – the reasoning behind it.

The reasoning is important, so don't make the mistake of skipping it as you will need belief if you are to withstand the inevitable losing runs on the way to the next winning cluster.

Today I have learned to make enjoying the racing the priority as well as running the site.

This book is written to save you 30 years of trial and error. I have done the work for you.

Not only that, but I want you to start enjoying your racing again.

My journey has been from casual, fun betting, punter, to stressed would-be pro gambler (in truth, more like semi pro) to well informed punter who approximately breaks even most of the time, has some bad days and some brilliant ones too. I enjoy them all.

Not many people have hobbies that pay for themselves.

That's where I want to take you.

If you want a guru, you are in the wrong place. This is not the definitive guide to backing horses. No such book exists – nor could.

This book is based on 10 years of blogs. My blogs work as a diary for me, and it serves you as well as me that I maximise their use.

Even if you are a pro, you should find something that improves your betting a shade (calculating your own going, for instance).

When you read on, you will enjoy either swearing at, or nodding in agreement with, what I have written on the principles. One thing is for sure – it will make you think.

Warning some of my views go against the grain.

Fundamentally, this book is aimed at those who love horse racing as their main hobby and want to enjoy their hobby at minimum cost and/or, with some luck – a big win that changes their life.

Almost every chapter has immediately actionable advice and I can guarantee this is not your usual horse racing betting book.

My aim with this book is not just to show you what to do but also why.

Knowing the why will keep you going when the results are going against you.

INTRODUCTION

Vindication! That was the overwhelming feeling as Tayarat landed the last leg of the 6-fold, shown below. No whooping, no dancing with joy – just vindication.

	Event Date	Event	Selections	Odds	E/W Terms	Result
1	20/09/2009	4.40 Hamilton (Win and Each Way) Live Stream RACING UK	Valid Point	6/5	3 Places 1/5 Odds	Won
	Best Odds applied, price updated to SP.					
2	20/09/2009	4.20 Uttoxeter (Win and Each Way) Live Stream AT THE RACES	Woody Valentine	16/1	4 Places 1/4 Odds	Won
3	20/09/2009	5.15 Ballinrobe (Win and Each Way) Live Stream AT THE RACES	Mutadarek	5/1	4 Places 1/4 Odds	Won
4	20/09/2009	5.30 Plumpton (Win and Each Way) Live Stream AT THE RACES	Tayarat	9/4	3 Places 1/5 Odds	Won
	Best Odds applied, price updated to SP.					
5	20/09/2009	4.30 Plumpton (Win and Each Way) Live Stream AT THE RACES	Shammy Buskins	9/4	3 Places 1/5 Odds	Won
	Best Odds applied, price updated to SP.					
6	20/09/2009	5.20 Uttoxeter (Win and Each Way) Live Stream AT THE RACES	Blossom King	7/1	4 Places 1/4 Odds	Won
	Best Odds applied, price updated to SP.					

Bet Type	No of Bets	Unit Stake	Stake	To Win	Returns
6 Folds	1	1.00	1.00	18,960.80	18,961.80

Total Stake: 1.00   Total Returns: 18,961.80

Figure 1 – Bet365 screenshot of Tayarat win and stakes

After all those years of snide remarks, "you're wasting time", "you're wasting money" etc – vindication.

And all those 'gurus' who said only 'mug punters' bet multiples – who is the mug now?

It got me thinking, did that near 20K win put me in lifetime profit or in loss? I had no idea and I didn't care. All I knew was I had an extra 20 Grand more in the bank now than I did in the morning.

All those years poring through the form books, burning the midnight oil. Yet the selections above took me around an hour to find.

No stress, no rushing, I had picked these the night before and placed the bets then too.

All I had to do now was watch them on TV.

"This is the life I thought", as I leaned back in my chair in the conservatory, where I was watching racing on AtTheRaces.

No betting bank, just betting what I could afford – and who can't afford a pound?

No calculating stakes from race to race. All bets placed the night before.

No searching out the best odds – though being sure to take Best Odds Guaranteed (BOG). All on with one bookie last night.

Only around an hour or so of research.

And I have just watched my one-pound win 6-fold pay nearly 18,962 pounds!

In short, living like a 'mug punter' and loving it.

What it really takes to be a pro gambler

I doubt you have been told this before...

Perhaps you too have had that dream. Professional gambler sat on the train going to the races. Laptop open, Racing Post too perhaps, finalising things before we arrive at the course and start organising the placing of bets for the gigantic coup we have plotted up and which will make us rich and famous.

Then we wake up! Professional gamblers, those who make their income solely from gambling are so rare that I doubt anyone reading this is one or will ever become one.

There are many reasons for this which are only partly to do with the personal attributes necessary to make a good living out of betting – patience, discipline, tenacity, money management skills etc. No, the fundamental reason that even someone who has the pre-requisites for success fails is for the same reason the majority of small businesses fail – under capitalisation.

Money makes money

Denman's former owner, and larger than life, big hitting, pro gambler, Harry Findlay, famously said that "No punter on the planet wins more than 8% of his turnover". P11 of Patrick Veitch's book Public Enemy Number One.

Let us suppose you could better that, and, to keep the maths simple, make 10% on your turnover. To better the average wage, to earn, say, £30,000 per year, you would need to stake £300,000 per year! Ten times your profit.

This can be done – at one extreme, by placing around £800 a day on one horse and, at the other, by backing an average of 20 horses per day to £40 stakes.

But where to find 20 good selections a day or £800? By the way, if you think that 8% profit is on the conservative side bear in mind that the great pro gambler, Alex Bird, worked on 2% profit and packed it in when 4% betting tax was introduced.

The other part of the capitalisation thing is cash flow. If you back as necessary to make a profit of 10% on turnover you will have a lot of of your bank tied up on an average day.

More than half your bank could be tied up.

Also, if you are looking for the best prices – and you should be – then you are going to have money tied up with lots of bookies.

You will surely be familiar with how it takes seconds to deposit money with the online bookies but a few days for it to appear back in your bank account!

Therefore, you really do need to have enough money to cover cash flow requirements, cover all the bets and to get the best prices.

So, while I do not want to discourage anyone who has the knowledge to make a profit, the cash to finance it all and the personal attributes (mainly the ability to keep at it through the inevitable losing runs – every famous pro I have read about had lost at least one bank – the winning runs are easy), I just wanted to introduce a note of caution so that anyone thinking of 'going pro' at least has some idea what they are getting themselves into.

Even as a hobby though, this can actually make you money

So, is it all a waste of time then? If we can't make a living out of racing why bother? Not at all.

First, it is fun. If it isn't, why do it?

Secondly, it isn't all or nothing. With at least some of the attributes listed above it is quite possible to supplement your income – some do!

Everyone has a hobby and, as I always used to tell my mates when I was on my way to the bookies and they on their way to the local pub on a Saturday, "I have a chance of walking out of the bookies with more money. Unless you hit the jackpot on the fruit machine, you will definitely walk out with less."

What's more this hobby could completely change your life

Ask Agnes Haddock who won £688,620 for a £2 Scoop 6 ticket based on names she liked!

Or the thousands of small stakes punters who took their share of the bookies' £40 million pay out on Frankie Dettori's Magnificent 7 accumulator at Ascot in 1996.

Of course, these are extremes, but I have had the big win I showed you, I should have won 30K a few years ago at Galway but for stinting on the perm just to save a few quid in stakes. I've also had many other 4 figure payouts. These examples are all to one pound unit stakes, by the way. Low risk – high reward.

Last Cheltenham (2021) I got a nice 1K treble up and would have had a 5K 4-fold acca had Windows Updates not taken my computer over for a couple of hours so I could not get the 4-fold bet on.

For the big win I showed you at the start all except the 16/1 winner came from the systems and strategies in this book. For the big festivals I use a mix of our portfolio and race trends.

In the next chapter, you will discover the motivation for devising the systems and strategies we now use. I hope they encourage you as much as they encouraged us.

In this chapter I will show you how and why we began to think we could become pro gamblers. The taster was a run of 19 winners out of 21 runners.

But first let me introduce myself so you can understand how my brother and I got into serious betting.

I am John Cutts and, along with my brother, Mark, we owned a small glazing company in Stockport, Cheshire in the UK before semi retiring to Brittany, France in 2012.

We are both in our early to mid-60's (only 15 months between us) and have been interested in horse racing betting since our teens (Red Rum, in the 1973 Grand National when I was 16, was my first bet and when that won, I was hooked – 25p each way!)

From those days up to the late 80's/early 90's we were Saturday punters who would pick our horses out of the Sporting Life then sit down at home or in the pub to watch the ITV 7 in the old days, and then Channel 4 Racing since 1984 and now ITV Racing.

In Autumn 1991 we were forced by economic necessity, (both of us landed up on the dole but Mark got a good redundancy pay off from the then CEGB – Central Electricity Generating Board for younger readers!) to find an alternative to wage labour.

Living in Greater Manchester at that time did not present many decent full-time job opportunities! So, we decided to try what we thought we knew about - horse racing betting.

We had read all those telephone tipster ads in the Sporting Life, and more importantly had made a most unlikely friend in our local pub – a chap whose brother was a vet and worked for several horse racing trainers at the time.

He gave us some fantastic winners that I still remember from all those years ago. Lochsong, (every time she won from the 1992 Ayr gold Cup at 10/1 onwards),

13

Branston Abby at 10/1, Palacegate Jack 14/1 and the Irish super mare Kooyanga when she won the 1992 Coral Eclipse spring to mind. Plus, many more.

Great days! And not only were we profiting from these and many more winners, so were our subscribers as, by then, we had several of them paying the odds to a fiver to our Racing advisory Service, The Inner Circle. (Mary Reveley's 1991 Cambridgeshire winner Mellottie which won at 10/1 just sprang to mind also, but enough nostalgia! Sniff.)

Our friend never bought a drink while we were in the pub, which was often, and he seemed to speed up when we entered!

We were making a half decent living from backing the horses and running the service, but all good things must come to an end and our friend's brother moved abroad and out of horse racing all together.

However, all was not lost as, during our Inner Circle phase, a bloke called Eric rang and asked would we like to combine our inside info with his placing bets for us using a novel method whereby losers were turned into non-runners (I will show you how to do this later in the book). The guy was a maths professor and a staking genius, but he couldn't pick winners to save his life. We teamed up – we provided the winners and he put the bets on.

Eric was a shrewd gambler who had all sorts of stake saving strategies. For example, instead of a Yankee, back 4 selections as 6 doubles but in a way that if any 2 win you not only get your double paid out at full odds but your 5 losing stakes returned as well!

We are going to write a separate Ebook/PDF on this, but the principles are exactly the same as we show for backing singles this way in Chapter 13.

When it is ready, I will send you the link to it, but you will need to be on our email list which you can join by copying and pasting the following link into the browser at the top of any web page: To learn this, go to: https://bit.ly/3HG7Zvb

If you are reading the paperback version, you will need to type the same link, exactly as it appears above, into your browser at the top of any webpage.

As a mathematician Eric's focus was on the bottom line and it did not matter to him which game.

He considered – very much against popular opinion – roulette to be the "straightest" game as there is only a 2.73% inbuilt advantage for the casino (in the UK). Whereas with horse racing you must overcome an overround of 1 – 2 per cent *per horse.*

Also, a 9% betting tax was in force then, which Eric got around by backing in doubles so that there was no tax to pay on the second leg.

Incidentally, I still use his roulette system to this day and have come home with more money than I set off with, more often than not.

He was also a keen racegoer.

Not long after meeting Eric, and collaborating on selections and staking, (with some success it should be said), he came back from Haydock with what seemed an incredible tale. He had met a man there who we have always referred to as "the London Bloke".

This guy was a multi-millionaire property dealer who made a lot of money on the side out of horse racing as a hobby, using a system for which he had paid £10,000 cash on the car park of that very same Haydock racetrack four and a half years earlier.

We still call him the London Bloke today – decades after we got to know his real name!

All of us, Eric included, were, to say the least, sceptical when he offered us a free trial in order that we would place his bets. We had nothing to lose though so we resolved to place the bets and keep a record for a month. We kept backing them for him (not a penny on for ourselves) and they kept winning.

It almost became boring to win in almost every race. "Lucky streak", "fluke", "they can't carry on like this forever", were some of the printable remarks we made.

But by the end of the month, he had backed 19 winners out of 21 selections! And one of the 2 losers was beaten just a head at 6/1 (Tutusixtysix, August 1993).

This was amazing, none of us had ever seen anything like it before, but the London bloke said 80% of the horses he had backed since he bought the system, four and a half years earlier, had won, and he didn't back odds-on.

We, for the first time, began to think we could make a living from just backing horses.

We were about to be educated!

Having cleared it with our new friend, we decided not only to back his selections but to place a half page ad in the Sporting Life offering, effectively, through post-dated cheque, a month's free trial.

Our new service was called Winners. We ended up holding around 50 post-dated £100 cheques. All we needed now was a repeat of last month and we would be earning £5000 per month (this was 1993) at least and our own winnings to boot! Some hope! The strike rate fell to 'only' 55% at an average SP of 11/10 and the cheques were returned.

My brother and I never got to meet the London Bloke. Everything went through Eric who was a little on the reserved side. I would have asked to have a look at his system to see if we could help identify a reason for the sudden fall in strike rate.

This was September 1993 and it coincided precisely with the 10lbs rise in handicap ratings for jumps horses that was introduced back then. It was the jumps horses that were letting the side down, falling from 80% to 45% compared to the flat which only dropped from 80% to around 70%.

It could have been a bad run. Even something with an 80% strike rate can have a bad month. But Eric would not hear of me talking to 'the London Bloke' so that was the end of that phase.

But we had seen it done. It *was* possible to achieve such results.

We were deflated yet inspired at the same time.

It wasn't just a good run. Eric got to know this man well over a couple of years and he was adamant that those results were not at all unusual and we trusted Eric's judgement implicitly. We had the bug more than ever now.

The last we heard of the London bloke was that the poor guy had a stroke and was in bad health. We later heard from Eric that he had died.

Eric, who was in his sixties when we met him, then died age 73 in 1999.

Since those days we have been on a quest to discover the rules of the system. The only clues the London Bloke ever left us were that he bought two papers a day, the Racing Post and the Daily Mail, the selection was the best horse in the race, and that when we discovered it we would kick ourselves because it was so simple.

In the mid – nineties, Mark and I set up in the glazing business (that is Mark's trade) so we had to research part time.

Now, I do not want to disappoint, so I must inform you that to date we have not discovered the complete system... but we have learnt an awful lot trying!

We have also discovered other systems during the search, which, though falling short of his stratospheric standards, still provide plenty of winners.

The most famous one is our Bet2 Win system, which we unveil in the next chapter.

Before that though, some acknowledgements to the inspiration for all our research since those days, the London bloke, and then of course Eric from whom we learned so much about maths, especially probability.

Eric pointed us to a book by Tony Drapkin and Richard Forsyth called The Punter's Revenge (1987) which was ground-breaking for its time in terms of using computers as a guide to gambling.

Then of course, DFL software who again broke new ground with their Compunter and Combayes computer selection processes.

These were an inspiration, no doubt, to the next generation at Racing Systems Builder (RSB) who came up with their seminal database and system builder of the same name, which, in my opinion, is unsurpassed to this day – and they started in 1985!

The Racing Post which is quite simply indispensable for the serious backer. If you don't believe me, try and get a serious bet on Betfair *before* RacingPostOnline puts up its betting forecasts!

Finally, since around 2010, when Racing System Builder closed, we have been using a site called HorseRaceBase for its system builder, amongst many other things. This has been a boon since the closure of RSB, closely followed by Adrian Massey upping sticks.

All these resources have helped us over the years. Not to discover the London Bloke's system (so far!) but to discover profitable betting strategies hopefully en route to its discovery.

After the London Bloke stopped, I was inclined to walk away. We had missed the boat. If only we had got to know the London bloke a few years earlier. However, Mark was spurred on to find out more, and, to his great credit, his perseverance paid off.

He analysed the list of the London Bloke's selections to see just what the London Bloke had meant when he said the selection is "the best horse in the race ".

You must remember that in those days – as we had not yet appreciated the full majesty of Racing Systems Builder – research meant thumbing through back issues of the Racing Post.

Anyway, he identified a few fundamental factors that would consistently produce the same selections as were on the London Bloke's selections list, but they were among several other horses.

There were rarely more than 2 or 3 selections per day. However, this achieved a strike rate of 48% at just short of break even at SP. We were onto something, but more research was needed.

Bear in mind we were now working full time in the Glazing business, so this process took place over several years. In between we would try and get an edge through vetting the selections on form, trainer stats etc and/or taking prices. The latter being revolutionised when Betfair set up in June 2000.

So, we had the basic ingredients but there were obviously more filters we had missed.

We had always wondered why he should mention that he bought the Daily Mail every day. So, one day in 2002 Mark and I spent a full day in Manchester Central Library looking through back issues, on microfiche, of the Daily Mail.

Here we made a breakthrough. We found a factor that increased the strike rate by 30%!

It took the strike rate up from 48% to 63% at an average SP of 11/10. Not quite "Eureka" as we had not achieved the 80% strike rate of its heyday and there were still some discrepancies – but far less!

This new system achieved a 131% return on investment.

This opened a new phase when we set up a new service call Percentage Betting to offer the selections from the system online to the general betting public over the Christmas holidays in 2003.

We were at the top of most search engines through the pay per click advertising medium of Google AdWords at that time. Plus, of course, backing them too. We were making a decent wage but not life changing amounts of money

Then we had a huge setback. In April 2004, the US government banned Google from facilitating the advertising of anything relating to internet gambling (I note the bookies ads are still up though!). So we had to change to full page ads in the Racing Post, Raceform Update, Racing & Football Outlook etc to promote the service.

These are not cheap and seriously dented our profits. We had a loyal clientele behind us however, and they got us through 2004 but we hit a bad run in November 2004 and ended up winding up the site by Christmas, a year after we started.

The system rarely performed up to the level it had previously achieved. There were some 8 winning months and 4 losing to level stakes at SP. The annual analysis showed a strike rate of 55% at 2.08, an ROI of 'only' 114.4%. Not to be sneezed at but disappointing by comparison with the past.

We still use this system.

When used with the Bet2Win System (next chapter) it provided the breakthrough referred to above – 63% strike rate at 131% ROI.

THE FAVOURITES SYSTEM

It really IS so simple you kick yourself.

Simply back the favourite in races where the favourite has won three of the last four runnings of that particular race. All races.

You can find these under 'Past Runnings on Racing Post online (minimum subscription necessary). Or, the Daily Mail, which shows the record of favs under each race. Three number ones in the last four, any order, and it's a bet.

This is the very thing we discovered in 2002 at Manchester Central Library.

As I say, we still use it but can't make any recent profits claims as we mainly back in multiples now and haven't kept a record of its results exclusively for a good while now.

All I can say is it used to make a profit (a 131% ROI at the beginning of 2004 that dropped to 114% ROI) by the end of the year.

We always put them in our multiples and we wouldn't be far from break even, by rack of the eye.

Having learned some lessons about blind copying of existing systems, the fact that even the best systems have a shelf life and the tendency for fluctuation – which means that both winners and losers can cluster in quite unanticipated ways – we have spent the ensuing years researching, backing and perfecting what we learned in our search for the 80% system of the London Bloke.

2004 was the year we took a greater interest in Racing Systems Builder.

We had a free copy (they used to send a CD with 2 years of data as a trial) which we had never really taken the trouble to get to know. We finally saved up and bought the 2 discs, one for jumps the other for flat.

These were an invaluable aid to testing all sorts of theories and a much quicker way to back-check systems (it is amazing how you start using something more often once you have paid good money for it!).

Through applying the lessons learned from our search for the London bloke's system and the knowledge we had acquired in so doing, plus the ability to instantly back-check any theories we might have – we have a flat disc that goes back to 1986–2009! – we have been able to develop our approach.

1. **Back horses that are the product of systems and methods that have a logical basis and have been checked in sufficient numbers and over a sufficient period to prove their worth.**

This was the lesson that led us to the BET2WIN SYSTEM and the Favourites System.

2. **Turn your money over – use leverage.** That is how the bookies bet and who better to copy than the most consistently successful?

All systems can be improved in terms of achieving a higher percentage strike rate and/or percentage ROI but this always means less selections.

Which means a much-reduced turnover. So, we have, at the average win rate of 40%, a preference for higher turnover.

Basically, money makes money and the only way the small punter has a chance of big pay days is by backing lots of horses either in singles or multiples which leverage your small starting stake. You should have a bank, as I will discuss later, but, if you haven't you can still cover small stakes multiples if it is money you can afford to lose.

I generally back an acca to one pound unit stakes.

On a Saturday or the festivals, I will cover the doubles too.

But if you can only afford 25p stakes you will still have plenty of fun finding plenty of winners that you sometimes catch in clusters for big pay-outs.

Failing that, the systems and methods I show you in this book will be useful for the ITV7 which is free and can win you 50K+.

I should do the usual sensible betting lecture here, but you are a grown up and, even just a quid acca on a Saturday isn't going to put you on skid row!

Besides, lots of people do the lottery and Euro Millions which offer little, if any, fun at all.

3. **Use Best Odds Guaranteed (B.O.G.).**

I know a lot of people play the exchanges and the best of luck to them. But we have found that we get better profits using BOG the night before racing.

BOG is simple. You take the price on the horse and if the SP is bigger, they pay you out at that bigger price. If, on the other hand, the odds shorten, then you get the benefits of taking the price and get paid at the price taken. We have found this gives us a real edge.

Ok. That's our biography in as far as it relates to horse racing, our philosophy and betting; the history of our search for the London bloke's original system; the discovery of it but at a lower performance than originally; lessons learned in the quest to find out that system and, finally, our approach today after 30 years of hard work and experience.

Here are the rules for the filter we discovered at Manchester Library:

<u>When combined with the Favourites System in the last chapter, this achieved the 63% strike rate at 131% ROI that our trip to Manchester library produced.</u>

The bookies seem to have got wind of it but it is still profitable and ideal for bankers in multiple bets.

We have never renounced betting singles, but we are always looking for the big win which, not betting big stakes, means a winning multiple for us.

You can get the selections from our portfolio every ITV racing day – The TV

Service. These will be system bets covered by ITV.

It's free and you also get the trends and selection for the day's big race.

These are every Saturday and any other racing covered by ITV such as the Cheltenham Festival, Royal Ascot etc.

CHAPTER 5 – Eric's Cluster Theory

"In the long run we're all dead"

That's what our staking guru and maths mentor said to me in response to my observation that his new roulette system might not work "in the long run".

Eric was a 24-carat character.

On the subs during the Second World War, he used to drive all the way from Portsmouth to Scotland the rare times he got back to Britain, to visit his fiancé.

I could write a short book about some of the tales he told me of those days – like when his dentist phobia led to him missing a plane ride that ended in a crash with all killed! Another time maybe.

For now, I would rather concentrate on the wisdom of what he taught.

This bloke had a degree in maths and engineering and, post retirement, he applied them to the cause of beating the bookies and the casino.

He used to virtually live in the casino in between slinking between bookies to get his bets on in the special manner that allowed him to turn losers into non-runners.

Despite being a liability, the casino manager liked Eric (he didn't play to big stakes – "under the radar" was his motto). One day he challenged the manager to a big bet.

He reckoned he could cover all 37 numbers on the table with 37 chips in such a way that he would make a 1 chip profit no matter what number came up! And if Eric said he could do it – he could do it.

When you consider the whole guaranteed profit for the casino is produced by paying 35/1 on a winning number when the real odds are 36/1 (37 numbers in total including the zero)

Let's put it this way, the manager never took him up on his challenge.

This was the basis of Eric's roulette system, but he also applied it to horse racing.

Using probability and a very sneaky (but legal and ethical) trick, he could stake so you turned losers into non-runners.

I will show you how to do that later.

Another of his was, instead of using one betting bank, he would split that bank into 5 or more, his reasoning being that winners would cluster dramatically in one bank and that bank would increase enough to more than make up for the other banks that didn't do so well or lost. Thanks to clustering.

Most of all it lent itself to backing winning multiples.

We are all familiar with the losing runs, but how many have noticed the winning runs? If losers cluster – so must winners.

It was what inspired me to go for the big win I show in the introduction.

Never mind STOP at a Winner – START at a Winner

Take advantage of those winning clusters and minimise the losing ones.

Just as, if you look at any set of results at, say, even money, you will see, from time to time, double figure losing runs, you will also see double-figure winning runs.

The same goes even for much lower strike rates. As an experiment, try waiting for a winner on your list of selections (horses, dogs, roulette, football, etc – it doesn't matter).

Only after one has won, back each of the next 3. If there is a winner, go again for 3. If no winner, stop and wait for the next winner then start all over again.

If you keep records, check back. You'll be amazed how it increases your strike rate and percentage profit.

There are three drawbacks for horse racing though...

1) You must be watching the racing (or at least the results) all afternoon – and evening as well in the Summer! Though you don't, of course, have to bet all day every day!

2) You greatly reduce your turnover as you are betting in far less races, which means your percentage profit may go up, but your cash profit could go down.

3) Because you are backing race to race, BOG isn't as big an edge – and it is near impossible to profit backing at ISP.

So, the strike rate will likely rise and the percentage profit too but the cash profit- the actual amount in money – will likely fall as far fewer bets would have been struck.

The simplest way to test the Cluster Theory is to flip a coin for a few minutes and record heads or tails. Choose heads as winners and tails as losers. The cluster theory will jump off the page.

This is the theoretical basis for betting multiples. Winning clusters are inevitable for the same reason as losing ones – distribution in maths language.

But how to use it to our advantage?

Here is the rarely mentioned reason you can't make your betting pay.

"Money makes money".

You have to be already well off or win a bank big enough to make a living out of.

To make something approaching the average wage as a pro gambler you would have to turnover around £300K PA.

Why?

You need to turn over your money

To quote the intrepid ex owner of Denman, Harry Findlay: "No punter on the planet wins more than 8% of his turnover." P11 of Patrick Veitch's book Public Enemy Number One.

Let's use 10% profit on stakes, or 110% return on investment (ROI), for ease of maths:

A 300,000 per year turnover would produce £30,000 annual profit.

This would mean staking an average of £5,769 per week, or £822 per day.

To make anything approaching the average wage, using a **selective** approach, you would need to stake **all** that £822, on average, every day.

And the bet/s would be on one or a few horses. Imagine putting 822 quid on one horse per day!

Now that IS putting all your eggs in one basket!

Even at a high strike rate, say 50% at odds of even money, it would be wise to have a forty-point bank and 40 x £82 = 32,880

Who has that sort of money to put to one side for a betting bank these days?

Without such a bank you wouldn't be able to turn over enough money to make a big enough **cash** profit to earn a substantial income.

Accumulate to speculate

You must win a bank big enough to make a living from before you can even start thinking about making a second income – let alone going pro.

There IS a way though that the small punter can eventually make big bets and thus have the chance of making a living. Turn your money over.

You can do this AND spend less time picking more winners

One of our systems in the portfolio allows us to Zoom in on the races most likely to be won by the form horse.

65% of the top two rated in these races have won over the past 25 years.

No overwhelm!

In those races, we can narrow it down to only the top two rated (never more – no joints or co's).

Doesn't it frustrate you when you spend all morning digging out what looks like a good thing only to find the price has gone?

A horse that you fancied and looked vastly over-priced in the betting forecast that has been backed off the boards by the time you try to back it!

Your typical racing day may begin something like this. You will check for clues such as trainer stats, race trends etc. You then use these to narrow the fields down to manageable levels for form study.

By the time you have looked at all these, your first race is half an hour away. You need to hurriedly make your mind up. You have precious little time for form study. You have rather long shortlist and little time to get your bets on and are often distracted.

By now, those over-priced horses you spotted have been discovered by others (not least the bookies).

They are now half the price they were. Very frustrating!

And who gains? That's right — the bookie. Of course, he has his minions to do all the research for him.

Let ACCU-RATE choose the races

Avoid the bookies' races. The ones where they offer to pay out on 6 places etc. By all means have some small fun bets on the big handicaps, etc, but save your serious bets for the ACCU-RATE races and the other system bets.

Narrow the field using ACCU-RATE

How would you like your typical racing day to begin with a look at the shortlisted races only? That would be just 3 out of the 36 races today. Then analyse the chances of the top two rated only.

Please note, though there are sometimes joint top rated, there are never more than two named top-rated horses. Unlike the big-name ratings services, there are no long lists of joint and/or co top and second top rated — always just two, never more.

In short: Accu-Rate narrows down dramatically the number of races to look at.

They then narrow down the field to a manageable size to study — just two in fact.

You save a ton of time and suffer much less stress.

Focus your time and attention on those horses most likely to win those races and get on early.

This means you can spend more time thoroughly studying the form, trends, stats between the top two rated in each selected race and can still get on early at Best Odds Guaranteed (BOG) without missing the best prices.

In fact, I can have my bets on the night before if the prices are up as I can start studying at around 6 – 7 pm, meaning I can get BOG prices early.

By the way, don't think that the high strike rate means only short prices either. We have had winners up to 14/1 and regularly get 5/1 winners and thereabouts.

Long winning runs and short losing runs

The high strike rate means more winners which, in turn, means longer winning runs and those frustrating losing runs are shorter. The longest losing run in the 25 years we have been using these ratings is 7 races.

Dutch them

If you get on the night before and use BOG, it is often viable to back each of the two selections by weighting your stake to make a guaranteed profit. Just google "dutching stakes calculator", there are plenty online.

Bankers for multiple and exotic bets

Also, because of the high strike rate, the winners tend to cluster. These ratings are excellent for use in multiples. You can use either both selections or choose one banker or do full or part permutations.

So, they can be profitably dutched or backed as singles.

You can use them for potentially big multiple pay-outs. If you choose the right races, you can get some very nice pay-outs on the Exactas.

Think outside the box.

There are many ways to use ACCU-RATE Ratings:

Perm them for multiples, as above. You can pick your bankers and, where you can't split them, put the pair in.

Perfect for exotic bets such as bankers for tri-casts, forecasts etc.

Good bankers for jackpots placepots, the Scoop 6 and the bet to nothing ITV7.

Even if you have no money to bet, you can use them for ITV7.

Another, for layers, is to make sure you are NOT laying these.

So, they can be dutched, backed as singles, for potentially big multiple pay-outs and, if you choose the right races, for some very nice pay-outs on the Exactas or forecasts.

These ratings will produce, on average, 5 or 6 races per day over the year. Though, on busy days like August bank holiday at could be in the teens and on a quiet Sunday it might be just one or two.

If you take the advice in the next chapter, you can compound winnings.

I have said before, and repeat again, that backing in multiples is just as valid a staking method as singles. The maths works out the same except, of course, the strike rate goes down and so, therefore, must the unit stake.

Kathleen has two even money selections. She has bet £1 win single on each. Both win, so her return is £4, giving a profit of £2 on the two bets.

Mark backs the same two horses but as a £1 win double. This pays a return of £4 – the same return for half the stake.

However, two will win 25% of the time (50% overall strike rate = 0.5, multiply this by itself and you get 0.25, or 25%), whereas one will win 50% of the time, or 0.5.

So, you can either win 25% of your bets at 3/1 or 50% at evens. In both cases you will break even.

Obviously, you need to adjust your stake to a quarter of that of your singles as your strike rate has reduced.

So, if Mark bets ten pounds win single on two winning singles for a stake of total stake of 20.00, that would return forty pounds, (20 profit).

However, if Kathleen wanted to get the same *cash* return backing the same two horses in doubles, she would need to stake 6.66 to make the same profit.

6.66 x even money odds = return on the first leg of 13.32. This runs on to the second winning leg at evens = 26.64 returns for the double, minus the 6.66 stakes = 24.98. Knock off the stake of 6.66 and her profit is 19.98 as near as damn it 20.00.

So, as you can see, the same horses backed in multiples, will pay just the same as if backed in singles, so long as the stakes are weighted to allow for the reduced strike rate.

Just a word on staking. It is best to back to round numbers. In the case above two x 10 pounds singles (twenty pounds) or a seven pounds win double would get past the bookies' radar.

They think if you are backing to what look like strange stakes, you are trading (backing and laying the same horse) which they consider their exclusive domain.

Excuse the maths lesson but there is something of a prejudice against backing multiples.

It is perfectly understandable. After all, the bookies have special slips for Yankees, Canadians etc and they wouldn't do this if it wasn't in their interest. You never, for example, see a special slip for a Round Robin.

Now I would not back Yankees etc. I stopped that years ago when our old mate Eric – who wasn't great at picking winners but was a wizard when it came to staking – assured me I wouldn't be kicking myself every time I got 3 winners if I just covered the 6 doubles and the acca. And you know what? He was right. I don't ever remember that happening over the near 30 years since I took that advice.

As he pointed out, the reason the bookies love these bets is that, to take the Yankee again, if the first one goes down you have lost 7 of your 11 bets – 63.6% of your total stake!

I could be accused of labouring the point, but it does seem to me that the recession, depression, slump, stagnation – call it what you will – has made this more than just an academic question.

And now we have Covid and all the economic fallout from that too plus inflation which mocks all investments.

In these times, how many ordinary punters can take the advice offered in the past by many (us included), to set aside, for a betting bank, money for betting only etc, etc.? That must sound like mockery to some now!

The truth is that most punters are backing out of their pockets. Perhaps they always were but even serious backers are doing the same now. Why? Because they simply don't have the money to operate a betting bank anymore. How many do?

The other thing that has changed, or rather exacerbated, is that more are looking for the big win. We pundits can talk to you about LSP's, ROI's, POT's, till we are blue in the face, but you want – truth be told we all want – that one big win that would make you financially independent. Or at least take the pressure off.

With all of the above in mind we can do one of two things. We can either (in vain in most cases) exhort you to patience and discipline, or we can try to help you in your quest for a big win – or at least some bigger wins.

Again, you can see a great example on the "My Big Win" screenshot – and there have been a number of smaller big wins.

That is what i think we are all striving forand we have had a couple of very near misses for 40 and 50 Grand wins since.

However, to achieve this you need good selections and sensible staking. We can help you with both these things. But, making this the aim and acting accordingly doesn't dispense with the need for patience and discipline.

These big wins don't come around often. What you need to make sure of, as I did on my big win day, is that you are there when they *do* come along. You must be still in the game. And you won't be if you throw the towel in after some inevitable losing run/s.

Now that the goal is set it is time to discuss how to achieve it. A lot depends on how many selections there are on the day. At the prices we generally back, we would need 7 or 8 winners for a high four figure win. If there are 8 or less selections, we will back them, one selection per race, in doubles and an accumulator.

For the reasons discussed above we don't try to cover the Accu-Rate selections in a full perm as that would cost us a fortune.

Equally we don't cover all the doubles, trebles, etc, etc, for 8 runners as that would cost us would cost £247 to £1 unit stakes!

Yes, (and it has happened a fair few times), you may get 6 winners from 8 and then wish you had covered the 6-fold but, believe me, it is almost certain you would have gone bust by then trying to cover all the perms each time.

Also, don't forget, in the 6 winners' case, you would have the winnings from 15 doubles for the 6 winners. This is the main idea of this staking. If you get all the lot up, great, you have a big win that can pay for a holiday, car, home improvement or whatever you want. If you fall short, as you almost always will, the doubles keep you in the game.

So, the lesson from this chapter is to not be afraid to shoot for the stars. You may never succeed but what will you regret most at the end? That one pound accumulator stake you put on every day or that big win you missed?

And I don't know about you, but none of us are getting any younger. I am 64 and long term, incremental bank growth becomes less appealing by the day. I want to win a big enough amount in one go and live long enough to enjoy it!

We cover all the daily portfolio in an acca every day to a one-pound stake and cover the doubles too when there are 8 selections or less or on a Saturday or ITV racing day. Don't forget to play the ITV7 using any of these selections too, as it is the best value bet going – a bet to nothing, infinity! The ultimate value bet!

If we are home, we often play the accas down so that, if the first one goes down we back the remainder in an acca for the next bet, and so on until the chance of a four-digit win has gone.

The lesson from this chapter is take all the selections you make using the systems and methods you learnt in this book to do a Daily one-pound acca at least. Or, if funds are low to a lesser amount, as you can afford.

What IS value?

First, what is the definition of value? There isn't one. The price of a horse is value if you think it is. That seems to be the theory.

On that reasoning, the whole field could be value as each backer would have a different opinion.

Some say make your own book, like a bookie would. Easier said than done! I hope you have plenty of time or you will be still doing it after the first race has started. That's before we start on having the necessary knowledge of maths – chiefly probability.

Others say vet your selections using value.

So, if everything else is right, check if it is a value price. Unless the horse wins its odds are of secondary interest. Only when the selection wins is anything **added** to the profit/loss calculation.

Others say back the price not the horse. But, especially on Betfair, the horses way out in the betting are almost always much bigger odds than the bookies have them. If you backed all of them, you would sometimes be backing 4 or more horses in the race.

You would hit some long odds winners, but you would have long waits between and you would need great faith as you waited for the next winner.

The argument goes that it is the value prices *over the long term* that provide the profit – but enough must *win* often enough to do so! And you need to be still in the game. Not short of money to bet with or quit because of losing runs.

What is 'the long term'?

And what is 'the long term'? Since you started betting? The last decade? Year? Month? Almost all punters could be super tipsters if they chose the right start date and end date for their example!

Whatever we call it, the decisive factor is that the odds paid must exceed the odds needed to recoup stakes. And for this to happen, the average odds must be greater than those needed to break even.

Or, put another way, your strike rate must be high enough to return more than your stakes. You could equally increase your profits by picking more winners at the same average odds.

So, for example, if Mark can achieve a 40% strike rate, his average odds must exceed 6/4 (2.5 or 40%).

However, that doesn't mean he would only back horses priced 13/8 and above. Greater than 6/4 is an average remember, not a minimum, which means some may be 5/1 or more while others could be long odds on (more on odds-on shots later).

This, I think, is a concept most backers find hard to grasp – **average** odds.

This will mean backing long odds-on as well as 5/1+ shots. If you don't, the strike rate will fall.

Equally, you could increase your strike rate to 50% at the same average odds,

You will get a lot of people who will say "I never back odds on". Really? Never? Even if Frankel was in a two-horse race over a mile?

I blame Pricewise! Punters have become accustomed to identifying value with a big price. But strike rate and odds are closely connected.

If Tom Segal's average winning price is 9/1, his strike rate will be 10% or thereabouts. This makes for headline grabbing news when he has a good run, but it must mean very long losing runs.

Probability tells us the chance of two consecutive 9/1 winners is 10 x 10 = 99/1.

Therefore, the chance of two such losers is 1/99 – ninety-nine to one on! By the way, I am not attacking Segal in the least, I think he is a top-class tipster. I am simply illustrating the mathematical chances which even someone as talented as Segal can only overcome to a limited extent.

However, clusters of winners DO happen – as I argue in this book.

A race versus a series of races – the 'experts' confounded by Frankie

One problem when examining value before racing has commenced is that a race is two things. It is an individual event, in and of itself. But it is also a part of the whole, a link in the chain so to speak. Thus, what happened earlier in the day affects odds in later races – form lines affected by wins or losses in the first races etc.

Think of Fujiyama Crest, the last leg of Frankie's Magnificent Seven at Ascot 1996, as the most dramatic example of this.

Forecast around 12/1 the horse was returned, because of all the multiple bets running up on it, the 2/1 fav with the race overround a bookie-consoling 150%!

No self-respecting value seeker would touch it with a barge pole at that price and any sane punter with money rolling up at SP, whose bookie offered cash out, (as they do today), would have grabbed the chance with both hands.

So, looking at that last race in and of itself, with such an over round, there was no value in backing the favourite. So, no play or back against it, as your original fancy will be an even better price.

But for the many lucky Frankie followers that day and for the 'gamble' followers whose motto is "a winner is a winner", that race was a success.

In the case of the Frankie accumulator backers – life changing!

People who knew next to nothing about backing horses made fortunes and us 'experts' were left scratching our heads.

They backed non-value horses in a way that is scorned – accumulators – and confounded the experts! Bravo!

Dumb luck? No, they had their own simple system – back Frankie!

So, there is also a context in which races are run which affects the price. A quick and logical way of assessing if your selection is a 'value' price

It must be 35 years ago now that I bought a book called Winners Always Back Winners, by Clive Holt. He was a pro gambler turned author then telephone

> *Amongst many other handy hints, the way he calculated value was simple and interesting. He calculated how many dangers, on all known form, there were, and then worked out the price he would accept from there. So, if he thought there were no dangers, he would want even money because he always allowed for "one from the field".*
>
> *If he thought there were two dangers, he would want 3/1 – the two dangers and one from the field.*
>
> *Clive Holt, "Winners Always Back Winners"*

tipster, Fineform.

That is the only time I have read a definition of value that made sense! I don't completely agree with it but there is logic to it.

That is the definition I would recommend as a sort of rack of the eye method but, as I say, don't make your perceived value price THE decisive factor. You will miss many good winners if you do and not necessarily increase your returns or ROI.

With his definition you wouldn't have backed the great Frankel all the 2011 flat season because you were afraid of a theoretical bogey man called "one from the field".

So, what IS the most important thing?

My contention is the most important thing is to find the winner.

If you think it is ridiculously short priced (a maiden winner in a Group 2 priced Evens, for example) leave the race alone. Don't back against it – any more than you would lay it – unless you are going to bet each way, place only, or bet without the av – if your fancy is favourite.

But, other than that, I make the priority picking the winner.

Which then is the most likely winner? The best horse in the race.

How do we find that?

We use the freely available information on the Racing Post site which employs a veritable army of experts to help you find winners.

When the professional odds compilers tell you the forecast favourite or second or third favourite (55% of the first 3 in the betting win) that is a pointer.

When their professional handicappers tell you a horse/s is top on Racing Post Ratings (RPR) and/or Topspeed these are kind of tips.

I am not saying back their information blindly, but I am saying use it to help shortlist.

This is dealt with in another chapter, but I didn't want to end this chapter on a bum note.

You can – and should – enjoy your hobby. Both the selection process and watching them.

First use the free systems and strategies in this book, then, if you need to narrow down, use the freely available information in the Racing Post to pick the best horse in the race (as far as we know). Finally, unless the odds look wrong by the rack of your eye, back it. If you back win only and the price looks wrong, skip the race.

The only advantage we punters has over the bookie is we don't have to bet in every race!

Finally, to sum this pick the best horse first vs look for the value debate, I was on a Zoom call recently, in the hot seat, trying to explain the above.

Two questions put me on the spot.

The first was, "I am eight years old and at the racetrack with you. Explain what we

> *So, to summarise, look for the best horse in the race, use Clive Holt's method as a rough guide – not the bible – to decide if that price is too short, if it isn't, back it – at Best Odds Guaranteed (BOG) if possible. If you consider it too short – don't bet in the race.*

are doing in one sentence".

After stumbling and mumbling for a minute I declared "The most important thing we can do in the next 20 minutes is pick the winner of the next race".

The second question was "If I am not looking for value, what am I looking for?" Again, to an eight-year-old in one sentence.

I replied, "You are looking for the winner. If the horse loses, its odds are not important".

CHAPTER 9 – Strike Rate and Losing Runs

Bank size

I have 'borrowed' the quote below from a blog by Kieran at **Make Your Betting Pay**.

Kieran says:

> "We need to strike the right balance between leveraging our profits and protecting the integrity of our bank.

> My usual starting point when carrying out this kind of analysis would be to calculate the longest expected losing run over 1000 bets. There is a formula for calculating this (mail me if you're interested) but I tend to use a table which makes life a lot easier. I've reproduced the table below (it's accurate enough for our purposes).

Strike Rate Percentage	Max Likely Losing Run Per 1000 bets
5%	135
10%	66
15%	43
20%	31
25%	24
30%	19
35%	16
40%	14
45%	12
50%	10
55%	9
60%	8
65%	7
70%	6
75%	5
80%	4
85%	4
90%	3
95%	2

Figure 2 – Strike Rate Table

The important thing to remember here is that the larger the number of bets you look at, the longer the likely losing run will be. As an example, with a 15% strike rate looked at over 1000 bets you are likely to hit a maximum losing run of 43 bets. However, if you were to have 10,000 bets with a similar strike rate, at some point you are likely to hit a losing run of 57 bets. That being the case, it's useful to have a reasonable idea of the number of bets your selection method is going to throw up over a period. If you are looking at a method that throws up 300 bets a year, then calculating your longest likely losing run over 1000 bets is ample. If you are looking at a method that throws up 10,000 bets a year, you need to dig a bit deeper than that.

Let's assume the method we are analysing has 1000 bets a year with a strike rate of 60%. We can see from the table that we are likely to hit 8 consecutive losers at some point during year 1.

You can see that if we were to choose a 10% staking plan on such a method, we are almost certain to hit trouble and quite possibly decimate our bank at some point.

We therefore need our bank to be several times the size of our longest likely losing run – it is well within the realms of statistical possibility that we could get 2 such runs in quick succession!

For safety, I would say it is best to work with your bank broken down into a number of points that equates to 5 times your longest likely losing sequence."

I heartily agree. There is no doubt that basing your staking on avoiding one long losing run is folly as it is more common that a series of losing runs is the bank breaker. Therefore, it is wise to allow for this.

Bet size

We tend to go for the higher strike rate/shorter odds selections. Why? Because the higher the strike rate, the more of our bank we can stake. We are also looking for winning clusters – multiples

Let's say we have a one-thousand-pound bank and a strike rate of 20%.

According to the chart, you could expect a losing run of 31 over a thousand bets. But that's not the whole picture. There will be many losing runs in the twenties and, as Kieran says, who's to say you won't hit (or beat!) the maximum soon after the first time!?

So, using Kieran's advice, your bank would have to be 5 x 31 = 155 points. Using a £1K bank, the stake would be £1000 divided by 155 = £6.45 and you could expect typically long waits between wins.

Our short price/high strike rate philosophy means one of two things. Either you don't need so big a starting bank, or you can bet a bigger proportion of a bigger bank.

To take the £1000 example. With a 50% strike rate we can expect a losing run of 10. Multiply by 5 and we have 50. Divide that into the bank of 1000 and our starting stake is £20.

Or, to take a different approach, we can back to £8 stakes from a bank of just £400, rather than a thousand. It is the same ratio.

We are a bit less conservative than Kieran. We use compounding and bet to stakes of 2.5% of the bank. After a winning day we up our stakes to 2.5% of the new, increased bank. After a losing day we reduce the stake to 2.5% of the reduced bank.

So, in a losing run, stakes automatically reduce. But in a winning run, they increase. This way we capitalise on winning runs but reduce losses on losing runs.

This also capitalises on the cluster phenomenon that our old friend Eric identified.

It is important, if compounding, to take money out from time to time, so as not to give the bookies the money back you have won from them.

You can grow your bank *and* spend some of it at the same time!

To recap: your singles stake is your expected longest losing run in a thousand bets multiplied by 5 (I would say 4 if you are compounding your stakes). Divide your bank by this longest losing run figure and you have your first stake.

Multiples staking

Add up your expected total returns from backing your horses in the bet multiple as singles.

Let's take an example.

We have 4 selections, and they are all 2/1.

If we put a tenner on each and they all win, the return will be 30 pounds (return for a 2/1 winner) x 4 winners = 120 pounds returned and 80 pounds profit.

If we want to make the same profit backing the 4 in an acca, we simply put a 75p accumulator on.

Just back the amount that will give you the same profit as backing the 4 singles by working out the profit if backed as singles.

The formula for this is:

Divide your total returns if backed as singles – in this case 120 – by the total singles stakes of 40 = 3.

Now divide this figure by the number of selections (so 3 divided by 4 = 0.75) and you have your stake that will give you the same profit as though you had backed your multiples as singles.

To check, simply multiply 0.75 x the accumulated odds (3 x3 x 3 x 3 = 81) and you have as near as damn it, the same return as you would if you backed the same selections in tenner singles. But, because your stake was only 75 pence, you make an extra 19.75 profit!

Psychology

This a greatly underestimated factor in betting. Some thrive on risk others prefer the more softly softly "I don't need the stress as I would like to live to spend the winnings" approach.

For even the most successful pro gamblers the odds and strike rate will not be too different. 50% winners at average odds of 6/5 would give a 120% Return on Investment (ROI) or 20% profit on stakes. Any pro would be delighted with that.

I know the average punter's dream is a selection method that produces a 30% strike rate at average odds of 8/1. But this is unheard of.

Even if a more realistic 15% winners at 8/1 was possible, almost no-one would have the belief and discipline to see it through. With a 15% strike rate, the chart shows 43 as the longest losing run to expect. How many of us would get to even half those losers before giving up?

Having surveyed our subscribers, we know these losing runs are their biggest bugbear.

Best Odds Guaranteed (BOG)

I read some time ago that only 20% of punters take advantage of the bookies concession Best Odds Guaranteed, (BOG). Therefore 80% of punters don't and are either taking Industry Starting Prices, taking a price with the Big Bookies, pitting their wits on Betfair or taking Betfair SP.

BOG is a pretty straightforward offer by most of the major bookmakers.

The name of the game for big bookies is to increase turnover mainly at the expense of other bookies or exchanges as part of a long-term process that will see, eventually, as with all businesses, the big fish eating the smaller fish by driving them out of business or buying them out. Therefore, every concession each bookie makes is aimed at boosting their turnover at the expense of their competitors to make sure they are doing the eating rather than being eaten.

Which, for now, is good news for us and we should make hay while the Sun shines.

What is BOG?

Best Odds Guaranteed is offered by some of the major bookies when offering prices for horse racing but not necessarily in all races nor in all types of bets. For example, some will offer BOG for singles but not for multiple bets such as Yankees etc. So always check the terms and conditions.

BOG is simple really. Before it came along – and it has been used on and off since the 80's to my knowledge – you could either take a price on a horse or take Starting Price (SP). In the former case, when the horse you took odds of 4/1 about romped home at 5/2, you would pat yourself on the back for your wisdom as you took the early odds of 4/1.

If the horse had drifted though, and won at 11/2, you were kicking yourself for taking the price because SP paid better than the early price offered. You could, of course, take SP, which would mean almost certain losses long term.

With BOG you are paid out on the best-case scenario. If the SP is greater than the BOG price you took when you placed the bet, you are paid out at SP. If the SP is less, you are paid out at the price you took.

Best Odds Guaranteed doesn't mean, by the way, Best-Ever Odds Guaranteed, as was explained to me in no uncertain terms by one of the ladies from Paddy Power's customer service team years ago!

If I take, say, 3/1 BOG price and that horse drifts out to 4/1 only to be backed in again to 10/3 SP, I will be paid at 10/3, NOT the best price that was ever available but the best of the two possibilities – taking a price and backing SP.

This is a marvellous concession and one we use for all our betting except for horses priced 20/1 plus where the betting exchanges have much better odds available.

Yes, there are Rule 4 deductions in the case of non-runner(s), but that is so if you take a price or let the bet run and accept SP.

Nowadays, we find the only reliable bookies when taking BOG the night before, is Bet365. Although this could have changed by the time you read this.

Racing Post Odds comparison site, Oddschecker, will tell you which bookies are offering BOG.

Why use BOG not the exchanges?

Pittsburgh Phil, on the excellent Flatstats site, did an excellent study regarding the performance of Betfair SP compared to Industry Starting Price (ISP) (which is decided by agreement between the big off course bookies now – hence the word "industry").

My saved link takes me to "page no longer exists', but I remember what I thought were the main lessons.

From this valuable piece of work, I note that Phil comes to similar conclusions to us regarding when it is best to use Betfair – for long shots.

What I find most interesting though is the 6.5% advantage that Betfair SP holds over SP for favourites. This is our experience, and not just for favs but the whole lower end, the 3/1 and under part of the market where most of the winners come from. It is why, as is said above, we use BOG bookies for all except the longshots.

Our experience is that, once you consider the Betfair equivalent to the bookies' Rule 4 – the reduction factor – there isn't much in it between the two. Therefore, anything that beats SP will beat Betfair SP.

I know from past, regular checks, that BOG has consistently outperformed Betfair SP when 5% commission and reduction factors are taken into account.

The only exceptions are with the long prices of 20/1+.

It also depends when you bet.

Research exists that shows that taking BOG around 8.30 the night before racing gives an ROI 7.5 times that of Betfair SP.

I am not able to link to the research but if you join our mailing list you will have my email address and be able to email me. I will send a link to the research by return.

You can sign-up by providing your name and email address on the following page:

https://bit.ly/3HG7Zvb

CHAPTER 11 – Long Odds-On Shots? The Fastest Way to the Poor House?

There is what can only be described as a prejudice against what are considered long odds-on shots.

Below are the results of backing horses forecast 1-2 or shorter from the start of 2010 to now (November 2021).

Bets	Wins	Win%	P/L(SP)	Places	Place%	Races	Race%	ROI(SP)
1845	1364	73.93	-55.1	1558	84.44	1845	73.93	-2.99

Figure 3 – Results of backing forecasts (2010 to 2021)

As you would expect, the strike rate is very high at 73.93%.

What is most remarkable is that, at SP, we lose only 2.99% on 1845 bets. This is almost break-even, which is amazing at SP and seeing as though received wisdom tells you it is the quickest way to the poorhouse.

If BOG is applied, this is profitable.

The cold, hard facts prove it.

Performance of System Overall and By Year

	Bets	Wins	Win%	P/L(SP)	Places	Place%	Races	Race%	ROI(SP)	P/L(BF)	ROI(BF)	A/E
ALL	1854	1371	73.95	-54.76	1567	84.52	1854	73.95	-2.95	-24.37	-1.32	0.97
2021	140	108	77.14	0.02	124	88.57	140	77.14	0.01	4.11	2.94	1.01
2020	128	94	73.44	-3.39	108	84.38	128	73.44	-2.65	0.51	0.4	0.97
2019	207	151	72.95	-7.67	176	85.02	207	72.95	-3.71	-3.32	-1.61	0.96
2018	203	145	71.43	-15.39	170	83.74	203	71.43	-7.58	-13.11	-6.46	0.94
2017	202	154	76.24	-0.63	174	86.14	202	76.24	-0.31	3.03	1.51	1
2016	199	147	73.87	-2.11	165	82.91	199	73.87	-1.06	0.5	0.25	0.98
2015	193	148	76.68	1.68	166	86.01	193	76.68	0.87	4.5	2.33	1.01
2014	203	147	72.41	-10.26	170	83.74	203	72.41	-5.05	-7.51	-3.7	0.95
2013	200	144	72	-10.75	163	81.5	200	72	-5.38	-8.37	-4.18	0.95
2012	176	130	73.86	-6.94	148	84.09	176	73.86	-3.94	-5.42	-3.08	0.98
2011	3	3	100	0.68	3	100	3	100	22.67	0.71	23.75	1.22

Figure 4 – Performance of system, by year

The above table shows what would happen at SP.

The final column on the right is the key as A/E means actual returns over expected returns according to the price – the market.

1 is break even, therefore any figure above 1 is profit, and any below, loss.

Even at SP, we make a profit in 4 of the 11 years. With just a small edge at BOG, every year would have been profitable.

At Betfair SP it loses just 1.32% on stakes over the past 11 years and shows a profit over 5 of the 11 years – including a 22.67 points profit for 2011.

So, why the sniffiness about long odds-on shots? Off that logic you would have admired the brilliant Frankel but never backed him once.

I assume it is the 'working man's price' thing. If the stake is fixed, say a tenner, a 3/10 shot doesn't look very appetising. And it's true, backed alone to a tenner's stake it will make you just 3 quid.

But imagine you backed it with one other horse. A 3/1 shot say, and it wins along with the 3/10 selection. If you backed them both as a double, you have effectively got a return of 52 pounds for the same ten-pound stake – 4.2/1 or 40% better odds.

Or imagine you get a 4-fold that pays 500 pounds. Had you included the 3/10 shot, you would have 649 pounds for the 5-fold.

Long odds-on shots (barring accidents) can enhance the odds of your longer priced winners when included.

Contrary to popular misconception backing horses forecast 1-2 or less in the Racing Post loses far less at SP than any other price band and breaks even or makes a small profit using BOG or Betfair SP.

What's more the very high strike rate keeps losing runs down and winning runs frequent.

Winning Sequences		Losing Sequences	
Sequence	Occurences	Sequence	Occurences
1	94	1	260
2	77	2	76
3	50	3	18
4	43	4	3
5	24	5	1
6	16		
7	9		
8	12		
9	10		
10	5		
11	5		
12	4		
13	3		
17	1		
18	1		
19	1		
21	2		
24	2		

Figure 5 – Winning and Losing Sequences, 2010 to Nov 2021

The above tables are for the same period as the others, 2010 to November 2021.

This is very much a system to have in your portfolio, especially as bankers in multiples.

RULES FOR THE SAVINGS SYSTEM

Back Any horse in any type of race forecast 1-2 or less in the Racing Post.

CHAPTER 12 – The Going's Good (Or is it?)

Along with the ability to get the trip, and, related to it, is the importance of a horse liking the going.

A horse whose optimum distance seems to be two and a half miles hurdling will often win a two-mile hurdle run in desperate ground. Usually, the jockey will put the pace on to expose any stamina flaws in his two-mile specialist rivals.

The reverse is possible. When the going is fast there is more chance of a two miler getting the longer trip in a slowly run race with a sprint finish - with this difference: while the jockey on the horse dropping back in trip can ensure a good pace, the one stepping up in distance cannot ensure a slow pace and it is often forgotten that (though the Cheltenham Festival illustrates it every year) you need to "stay", to last home, even over 2 miles on Good to Firm.

It is not unusual for horses considered stayers to win at shorter trips, especially in the handicaps if the pace is on – and the pace is always on at the Cheltenham Festival!

In short, it is easier for a "stayer" to drop back in trip if the going is Soft or worse and run at a fast pace, than it is for a "classy" speed horse to step up in trip in those same conditions. In the latter case the horse would be greatly assisted by both fast ground and a slower pace in which it could show its speed.

Just a couple of examples from memory:

One Man won the 3 miles King George Chase at Kempton on Boxing Day and, after failing to get home up the hill over the 3m 2.5 furlongs of the Cheltenham Gold Cup, dropped back in trip to win the then Queen Mother Chase over 2 miles at the Cheltenham Festival.

The great Istabraq was beaten by Martin Pipe's awkward squad stayer, Pridwell, when he tried to step up to two and a half miles in the big Grade 1 hurdle at Aintree in a real bog.

The following season this 3 times Champion Hurdle winner won the same race on better ground. By the end of his career, he had notched up four Grade 1 hurdles over 2m 4f plus.

So, he got the trip ok. It was just the going at the distance, a fast pace on the ground and a master ride from AP McCoy that day on the famously awkward, but classy on his day, Pridwell, that beat him (by just a head) showing the above observations apply even to the all-time greats!

The course is another matter and one that whole books have been written on. It is the third consideration for me when looking at form. Although, the type of course is related to the ability to stay and some courses are 'easier' than others.

I never forget John Francome correcting one of the Channel 4 team when they said such and such a horse would find it easier to last home over the King George trip of 3 miles than at Cheltenham.

Francome explained that, even though Kempton is a flat sharp track, or perhaps just because of this, they are able to go at breakneck speed which makes stamina come to the fore in the closing few furlongs as they have gone off so fast.

No wonder someone once described Horse Racing as "the glorious uncertainty!"

So, you can see why we punters need accurate information to make an informed decision. The distance is a constant. Same too the courses. Barring the odd cock up, moved rail, or fences removed because of low Sun, of course!

If a horse is proven at the distance at or on a similar course, then there is only one other factor to consider barring horse, trainer, and jockey form and records at the course, etc, etc.

One factor that is constantly changing and that is **the going**. It is this factor to which this chapter is devoted. It is the least constant, most inconsistent factor in the big four big form considerations of class/distance/going/course – and it is the hardest to assess as official goings are often wrong, as proven by the race times.

All the above assumes the horse is running in its class – the most important factor of all. This can only be taken as read if your possible selection has won or gone close in the same class.

Who decides what *the going* is and how?

The Clerk of the Course decides having walked the course, probably for days ahead and more than once that morning early on. He must report the going to the Racecourse Association who then pass on the news to the press.

Since March 31st, 2007, something called the going stick (penetrometer) is used to give a number between 1 and 15. The nearer to 1 the softer, the nearer to 15 the firmer. It is mandatory for all UK race courses to carry out these tests and for the British Horse Racing Authority (BHA) to put the number next to the going description.

Frankly, I don't trust these going reports. A man weighing perhaps a couple of hundred weight is no comparison to a horse weighing over half a ton, or 10 plus hundred weights (500kg+), walking around.

Also, I would have thought the old stick test would depend on the weight, strength and effort put into it.

To be fair it is very difficult to have any objective, accurate idea of the going without knowing the race times and I am afraid that, for all my criticism of this old-fashioned method, I don't have a better idea.

The whole thing with going can be tricky as you can have softish ground under a good covering of grass which can sometimes ride fastish and record fastish times.

For me, what is important is, not the tag we give the going, but whether the going suits plodding stayers or those with gears and a turn of foot.

One trainer put it well when asked if his horse would mind the soft ground and he replied that it would help his horse in that it would slow the others down!

So, logically, we know the distance and we know the type of course but, until at least one race, (usually a few), has been run, we don't know if the ground suits the speed horses or the plodders.

Would you bet without knowing the race distance? Nor me, yet we bet with nothing much more than educated and sometimes self-interested guesswork informing us of the underfoot conditions.

It is necessary to understand that course representatives are loathe to put extremes of going into their descriptions.

When did you last read it was Hard at Brighton, which it was often described as in the past? How often is the fastish ground we are seeing at Cheltenham, and which is sending course records tumbling each year described as Good to Soft?

Also, Soft (Heavy in places) is becoming more common.

This is understandable. All sports are businesses nowadays and they want to attract as many runners as possible. So nice, in between, descriptions of the going stop early defectors and, once the connections are there, they will generally reason that they may as well give the horse a run anyway.

How to calculate *the going* for yourself

We calculate the going according to the race times in comparison to the Racing Post Standard.

The basic formula is to divide the number of furlongs of the race into the number of seconds slower than Racing Post standard time. This is the figure in brackets by the number of furlongs. This is shown in brackets after the race time, at the bottom of the result for that race on the results page.

There are two ways to do this, one of which is much quicker but not quite as precise as the other, which I will go into later, but first it is important to understand how the figures are arrived at.

The fundamentals

For the fastest method and most accurate record of race times, you need to click on "Racing Post (RP) Members Club" and select a package, if you haven't already got one.

The minimum "Essential Membership" will do for our purposes. However, as long as you understand the fundamentals, I will show you a way later to calculate the going for free, just your own effort for less than a few minutes with a calculator. Maybe not quite as precise as the RP figures but very close to them.

First, I will explain and illustrate the fundamentals. The example meeting will also show how inaccurate the official going can be.

The meeting and the race I examine are from a few years ago but the arguments are as valid now as they were then.

Once on the Racing Post's Horse Racing home page click on the "Results" tab, scroll down until you reach the meeting you are interested in, click on it and scroll down until you see "ANALYSIS OF WINNING TIMES" where a page like this should be displayed (on the left of the page halfway down).

Haydock   22 Nov 2014

RACE	WINNER	RPR	DISTANCE	TIME / PER FURLONG	COMPARISON / PER FURLONG	TS	TS BASED GOING	OFFICIAL GOING	GOING CORRECTION
12:10	Vasco Du Ronceray >	141	1m7½f	4m 0.50s 15.36s	+22.50s +1.44s	—	—	Soft	—
12:45	Gas Line Boy >	147	3m4½f	7m 44.30s 16.33s	+21.30s +0.75s	—	—	Soft	—
1:15	On Tour >	140	2m3f	4m 51.30s 15.44s	+25.30s +1.34s	—	—	Soft	—
1:50	The New One >	164	2m	3m 57.30s 14.64s	+11.30s +0.70s	—	—	Soft	—
2:25	Aubusson >	155	2m7f	5m 53.00s 15.48s	+19.00s +0.83s	—	—	Soft	—
3:00	Silviniaco Conti >	175	3m	6m 10.70s 15.38s	+3.70s +0.15s	—	—	Soft	—
3:35	According To Trev >	138	3m	6m 24.30s 15.94s	+17.30s +0.72s	—	—	Soft	—

Figure 6 – Racing Post Analysis of Winning Times

The Racing Post has a standard time for each race distance at each track in the UK and Ireland and some of the big races away from the British Isles.

The figure in the fifth column, the one after the DISTANCE, headed TIME/PER FURLONG, shows the time for each race run and then that time broken down into seconds per furlong.

Once the first race has been run, it is possible to view the COMPARISON/PER FURLONG (the figures in the next, the sixth, column).

So, if we look at the first race at Haydock on the above card, it tells us the race had been run in a time 15.3 secs per furlongs slower than standard time for a race of that distance (the figure next to the race time on the right).

Next to that on the right is the time per furlong above standard. It is the result of dividing the total number of seconds above Racing Post standard time (plus 22.5 secs in this case) by the number of furlongs (15.5).

This gives us a time of slow by 1.44 seconds. It was run on the hurdles track and was the slowest time of the day.

This is the best guide to the going. How many seconds per furlong above Racing Post standard time the race/s were run at on that track on the day.

When you gain confidence in this, you can just use the time per furlong. In this case, 1.44 seconds per furlong below the standard Racing Post time.

That, fundamentally, is all you need to know.

1) The number of seconds above standard for the race. 22.5 in our example

2) Divide this by the number of furlongs, in our example 15.5 furlongs, and you get the seconds above standard per furlong.

So,22.5 divided by 15.5 = 1.45

This is the rating, 1.44 seconds (you will never get a perfect match but 0.01 secs is nothing) per furlong in the example race above,

If you take away the decimal point, this looks pretty similar to a scale that an outfit called Superform used to use.

Superform were a sort of poor man's Timeform, although, having tried them both, I always preferred – and used – Superform.

Unfortunately, the digital age proved a step too far for them and they are not around anymore. But their time-based going figures live on!

They assessed the going by adding the time per furlong figures from the first 6 races, (I use the 6 fastest to allow for the odd small field dawdle).

So, using my method, (the fastest 6 races), the going at Haydock on Betfair Chase day was, using the 6 fastest (excludes race one which was the slowest run on the day):

+0.75	+1.34	+0.70	+0.83	+0.15	+0.72

NB, **this is for the fastest 6 times and therefore doesn't include the first race,** which we analysed above.Add the 6 together and it comes to 4.49 secs. Now divide the total seconds per furlong above standard by the number of races to get the average of slower than standard by 0.75 seconds per furlong.

So, what does this tell us about the going?

Superform worked out a scale on a very similar basis. I am working from memory here I am afraid because I long since lost my old Superform annuals in 2006 when we moved to France first time. But it went like this.

Exactly standard time, which would be written as 00.00 in brackets under the race times, or less = HARD

+01 – +0.20, (which they expressed as 20 – using only the figure to the right of the decimal point) = FIRM

+0.21 – +0.4 (21-40) = GOOD TO FIRM

+0.41 – +0.8 (41-80) = GOOD

+0.81 – +1.2 (81-120) = GOOD TO SOFT

+ 1.21 – +1.5 (121-150) = SOFT

+1.5 upwards (151+) = HEAVY

So, we can see that by these criteria, the going at Haydock on Betfair Chase day was on the slow side of GOOD (75) – nowhere near the official going of Soft (Heavy in places).

The At a glance method

Ok, having looked at fundamentals...

There is some debate about what produces fast times. Obviously the faster the pace the more reliable time is as a guide. Also, it is possible that a good grass covering on top of firm-ish ground could produce a springy surface. Apparently, on the U.S. dirt tracks, there are often fast times clocked after it has rained heavily!

However, fundamentally, we are looking for whether the ground suits stamina laden horses that just stay on, or speed laden ones that quicken. The labels we put on such conditions are only useful if they offer guidance on that score.

Ok, having looked at the basics, let's now study the times using an at-a-glance approach by having a practice on the Betfair Chase which was run at Haydock The official going was Soft. If we were planning a bet on the day at this track, it would make sense to keep an eye on the time for this first race. Now we can go straight to the, (let's call it Goingform), figure, the one on the right under the heading COMPARISON/PER FURLONG

You can see that Vasco Du Ronceray wins the first race in a time of 1.44 secs per furlong slower (144 or Soft) than the standard Racing Post time. This would seem to confirm the official going.

But the second race was won in a time just 0.75 secs slower than Racing Post standard times, which would suggest Good going!

Sometimes too, the hurdles course can be on the slow side and the chase course on the slow, and vice versa.

The first race was a hurdle and produced the slowest time per furlong of the day at Haydock. The second was a chase.

In fact, the chases produced 3 of the 4 fastest times of the day.

As I said earlier, pace can have a big effect and maybe the first race was run at a snail's pace and the second was truly run.

If you have been looking for mudlarks all the previous evening and that morning, you have been wasting your time and the alarm bells should be ringing! This bit of knowledge alone could save you a fortune in bets *not* placed.

We already know the average 'Goingform' rating for the meeting was 75 for the six fastest times but, now we know the reasoning, there is no need to go through the whole procedure. We can simply look at the Goingform figure's to either get an idea of the going as the racing proceeds, note any seemingly fast times, or add the figures together in our heads or with a calculator. If you knock the decimal point off it is much easier.

Talking of looking at individual race times and ratings, note the time of SILVIANACO CONTI's race, slower than standard by 0.15 secs per furlong or 15. This would mean either the going was Firm, which is highly improbable, or the first two home are very smart King George contenders.

The fast time also tells me any issues MENORAH had with a stamina test were down to his breathing problem which has been corrected by a wind operation. This is the sort of analysis you can make when you know the actual going rather than the official going.

Wouldn't it be good if we could know this in advance? We can and did. We told readers of our blog that the going was nowhere near Soft and tipped up MENORAH, a none too certain stayer on the alleged bog, which finished second having been backed from 16/1 into 10/1.

How did we know? Because there was racing at Haydock the day before which enabled us to evaluate the race times and make our own judgement about the going.

This is the ideal scenario. Day two or more of a meeting is best because you can monitor the going as the races progress so that you won't be picking mudlarks running on Good going or speed horses running on Heavy. You can then spend the evening and some of the morning looking at those which will relish the going giving you time to get the early BOG prices.

This is ideal for the big festivals like Cheltenham and Royal Ascot etc.

But, if you have the patience to sit out the first 3 or 4 races, it will give you a real edge in the later races where, often, everyone is labouring under the illusion of the official going

Rack of the eye method

Once you get used to this you can do what we do which is use the rack of your eye, do the maths in your head, or with a calculator. If the official going is Soft and the first race is run over 2 miles (16 furlongs) in a time 8 seconds slower than standard, it is not hard to work out that 8 seconds divided by 16 furlongs equals a race run 0.5 seconds per furlong slower than Racing Post standard. Slow by a Goingform rating of 50, which, if you check on your scale above, is Good.

The beauty of this is it doesn't cost you anything. If you sit there with a calculator or pen and paper, you can work all this out without spending any money on a Racing Post package by simply remembering that the key figure for each race is determined by the number of seconds it was run above standard divided by the number of furlongs. Then remove the decimal point to get what I have christened the Goingform figure and check it against the scale above.

Conclusion

You will never have the excuse again of blaming the newspaper for giving you the wrong going! I don't say this method is anywhere near perfect — not least because of the weather changes - but it does indicate, better than any other I have seen, the approximate likely going.

Unlike the official going, which is regularly miles out, you should be thereabouts using this method — though beware of small fields and/or slowly run races which are not unusual nowadays.

How many times have you had two short-priced fancies and wondered whether to put them in a double or back them in singles?

And then, how many times has one of them got beaten a short head? And if you covered the double, that's down as well!

Here is a way around that. This is a way of doing the same bet but covering against the possibility of the first or the second selection losing.

YES, YOU READ THAT RIGHT!

Figure 7 – Betting slips

The race meeting times are just to illustrate that you are not obliged to bet in real time but can bet in reverse time. The betting slips above are self-explanatory.

What isn't evident to the untrained eye is that if one of the horses wins and the other loses the £10 losing stake is returned because the £1 win bet stops the second bet as our instruction is 'If Lose' – thus turning it into a non-runner! Let's examine what happened with this real bet.

If Mark bet conventionally, 11 pounds win on each, he would have staked £22 and received back £16.50p – a loss of £5.50p.

Backing as above - using either "if lose" or "stop at a winner" (SAW) – they are the same thing – would make a profit!

Two points staked and one and a half returned –how?

Taking the William Hill bets first: £1 win STAND GUARD – wins at 1/2, returns £1.50.

The £10 bet on the ABARTA is stopped because you have stipulated that it becomes a bet only if STAND GUARD loses, which it hasn't.

Hills return should pay £1.50 for the £1 win single on STAND GUARD plus £10 returned stake for the, now void, bet on ABARTA.

TOTAL HILLS STAKE = £11, TOTAL RETURNS = £11.50 (see settlement slip below). Profit = 50p.

But if you had placed this bet conventionally, without the "if lose" stipulation, you would have got £1.50 back for STAND GUARD but lost a tenner on ABARTA giving a loss of £9.50 on the total bet.

On the Ladbrokes slip:

The £1 win bet on ABARTA is lost but this now means the second leg, (note, not second in time order but in the order on the slip, which is how the bet will be settled), is live.

STAND GUARD becomes a bet only if the first named loses and it does in this case. So, we have lost £1 on ABARTA but this means our tenner on STAND GUARD goes ahead and this wins at 1/2 giving us a return of £15.

TOTAL LADBROKES STAKE = £11 TOTAL RETURNS = £15 (see settlement slips below). Profit = £4 which is the same as if backed conventionally.

```
William Hill Results    23 Aug 2011 15:53:51

SLIP            STAKE      TRK    TOTAL  STRUCK
561702627730    11.00      0.00   11.00  8 Aug 2011 14:18:59

Unknown                Section Stake: 11.00

SLIP RETURNS     VOIDS            TOTAL
      1.50       10.00            11.50
```

```
                              Ladbrokes

Payout Confirmation

Shop number  :  2412
Reference number  :  9487195997
Taken on  :  08/08/2011 14:11:46
Total slip stake  :  £11.00

Payout date  :  23/08/2011 15:52:20
Total return amount  :  £15.00
```

The benefit of backing this way can only be appreciated though, when you take the two bets together, as one: The advantage is £11.50p.

A point on two singles at level stakes, with just one winner at 1/2 has produced a profit of 1.05 points! This is gone into in more depth below and is worth examining as it looks at cases where both-win or both-lose.

Many reading this will know how to, or at least have heard of, Stop at a Winner bets or SAW for short. But I will be surprised if one in a thousand knows that you don't have to back in real time or race time order.

You can back in reverse time order and that is how.

Just check the terms and conditions of the remaining bookies who still offer to take conditional bets.

They say a picture is worth a thousand words so here is an example of what I am talking about. It is an alternative to backing two short-priced selections at, £10 each in two singles.

The example below is simply a different way of writing the same bet as on the betting slips above. "If lose" is the same bet as "stop at winner".

BET 1	BET 2
2.30 LIN £1 win A	3.30 LIN £1 win B 3.30
LIN £10 win B 2.30	LIN £10 win A
SAW*	SAW

* SAW means stop at a winner.

Figure 8 – Alternative wording for above bet

A 50% strike rate is ideal for this staking plan so let's assume each selection is backed at Even money (or 2.00 for younger readers!)

SAW means stop at a winner. A 50% strike rate is ideal for this staking plan so let's assume each selection is backed at Even money.

If you compare this to having the same amount on each selection you can see this is a much better option, where only one of the selections wins. Putting £10 on each would cost £20 and return £20, it would just break even. Splitting the bets up into tenners and quids allows us to use the small stakes as "enabling bets":

They enable us to stop the bet on the second leg even if it has already lost.

I look at that as an insurance premium against one being beaten.

I am not claiming that this will make you rich

Nor necessarily in the long run will it pay any better than backing at level stakes.

No staking plan can, in the long run, compensate for a selection method that doesn't make a profit at level stakes.

The same method that stops the losers will stop winners too!

In our example above, if both win then we merely get our money back plus £1 profit off each enabling bet. If A wins it stops BET 1 and if B winning stops BET 2. So, a profit of £2 is all that is achieved. Which seems a waste of winners!

However, bearing in mind all the tenners we have saved, we can afford to cover this eventuality by backing the double.

The saved stakes 'buy' you the chance to have a crack at the double! The maths is that there is a 3/1 (25%) chance of two even money shots winning in any sequence of 2 selections. Basically, there are only four ways a bet involving 2 horses can play out and the chances of this happening are governed, in the long run, by the strike rate.

So, at Even money, there is a 25% chance of each of the following sequences happening: WW, WL, LW, LL. As you can see, just the one winner should happen in 50% of cases – WL & LW.

Both losing, (in which case you are in the same boat as backing to level stakes), should happen 25% of the time and WW should happen in 25% of cases.

Bear in mind though, that for all WW makes up only 25% of sequences it contains half of all winners. Therefore, it makes sense, to devote 25% of your stake less the 'insurance' bet, to the double.

In the above example we would cover the double to a stake of £5.

The figures would stack up like this:

Bet 1 Because A and B have won you get £2 returned for your £1 win bet on A but this stops the second, (winning) bet on B which returns only the stake. Total returns for Bet 1 = £11

Exactly the same happens in Bet 2 = £11 return

£5 win double on two Even money shots return £20 Totals £27.00 staked (2 x £11 from each singles bets + a £5 win double) £44.00 returned (£24 from the returned single stakes and £20 from the double) Profit =17.00

To summarize, backing in the above ways ensures a profit in all cases (75% of the sequences of two selections, backing Evens shots), except where both lose. And 100% of the occasions where there are one or more winners. Whereas, at level stakes, you would need both selections to win to show any profit at all.

What is unique with *this* way of backing is that you can change your losers into non-runners even *after* they have lost.

Even if your first horse loses, you can still profit with only an even money or even a long odds-on shot running for you. At the time of writing, they all stipulate in their rules that bets are settled in the order they are written. Or, in the case of telephone bets, in the order they are read out.

Unfortunately, I know of no way this can be done on the net.

I recommend the staking ratio of 1 to 10. You could make the enabling bet 10p but the bookies will simply stop accepting your bets – this has happened to us. As our local Hills bookie put it "It's not worth me bending my back to keep giving you your 10p's back!"

You should be ok with £1 to £10. If you have a good run, it may be a good idea to go elsewhere for a while. These are tactical ruses which you will learn as you go along but keep your local bookies sweet

And don't forget, this can be done with multiple bets too using the same "if lose" method.

There are numerous ways this method can be used, one of which is a stake saving alternative to the Yankee.

When you join our mailing list, you can email us for how to do this and we will send you the instructions - free.

You can join the mailing list on https://bit.ly/36As7ll

Why do we bet? Everyone will look bemused and say, "to win money, of course" But is that true?

Obviously, people want to win money but is that the sole reason? Is it not to be right – vindicated, as I put it in the introduction? To have solved the puzzle?

And how about the thrill as they turn for home? The adrenaline rush when yours is still in contention on the run-in? And that feeling of vindication again when it passes the line first?

That's why it is our hobby. That is why it gives us so much pleasure.

It is thrilling. But it can also be stressful.

Who hasn't withstood the harrumphs, the heavy hints, the yawns, as their other half paces up and down waiting for them to help do the shopping on a Saturday morning?

It is very difficult to pick winners in that atmosphere where the choice is shopping or concentrating on picking your horses and getting your bet on.

The solution? Use the above systems, tips and strategies I have supplied so that you can have your selections picked and the bets on in an hour or so the night before.

It is not unreasonable to want to get the shopping done, nor to get your horses picked and backed. Problem solved.

Almost all the stress of Saturday racing removed at a stroke.

That is one of the aims of this book – to make betting fun again.

Another aim is for you to set your expectations realistically – hence the chapter that outlines "what it really takes to be a pro gambler "

This is a further reduction in stress as you accept that your prime reason for betting is for pleasure and not to play at being a pro gambler.

Does this mean abandoning all hope of profit? Not at all, just a different way of making it – hence the chapters on multiples and the systems to use for the selections for those multiples.

And there is no law saying you can't use the selections to help you make a level stakes profit backing singles. If this book has given you one idea about how to bet better, then my job is done.

But the title of this book is 'Lose less" and that is the main aim.

It seems to me a good idea to learn to walk before learning to run. If you can do that and then want to put the time and effort into building a betting bank, why not? Hence the chapters on bank management, stake proportions etc.

https://bit.ly/3HG7Zvb

Losing less may seem such an unambitious aim, but it could save you thousands of pounds a year – simply by NOT doing other things! If someone is losing 50 pounds per week, that is 2600 pounds per year. If the information in this book only halves that, then you now have a hobby that costs half as much as previously and have saved 1300 pounds.

This can be achieved by utilising the Cluster Theory whereby winners cluster as do losers – hence the concentration on the top end of the market, in general, for our portfolio, as such clusters will be more common and the gaps between them shorter.

The aim is that you are a less stressed, more contented punter, with realistic aims (not constant frustration and disappointment), who bets, generally, horses at or near the head of the market, at small stakes, in order to land winning multiple bets. These can be winning doubles right through to 10+ fold accumulators.

Taking this approach should improve your close relationships too in buying you more time.

How to Apply What You Have Learned in This Book

I would advise against throwing yourself into it.

Keep this book for reference, print it out if you have the Kindle version or buy the hard copy by going to this page:

https://www.amazon.co.uk/dp/1732993998

I would advise you start with Bet2Win as this is likely to provide the most sole selections.

The rules for this system are at the end of chapter 4.

After a week add the Favourites System which is at the end of Chapter 3.

You will then have the system we used for a year that ended up achieving a 55% strike rate and a 114% ROI.

The next week, add the selections from the Savings System, the rules for which are at the end of Chapter 12.

I would then stick with these 3 systems for a month or so, till you can make your selections very quickly, before moving on to Accu-Rate which will take a bit longer to find the selections and will mean experimenting how best to use them for your purposes.

Finally, don't forget to join our mailing list at this address:

https://bit.ly/36As7ll

As a list subscriber, you will be entitled to free selections from our system portfolio for the ITV races each Saturday and any other day they are on ITV – e.g., Cheltenham and Royal Ascot.

You will also receive the race trends, shortlist, and selection/s for the big race of that day.

You will automatically be mailed with them, sometimes the night before – sometimes the morning, of racing.

This will make sure we keep in touch, and you can contact us with any questions or comments, and we can write to you with anything related to the subject of this book that we think may interest you.

If you have found this book interesting, please refer to a friend.

Also, feedback is always welcome, and you can provide that by leaving a review on Amazon, at the following link (simply scroll down the page and you will see ":

https://www.amazon.co.uk/dp/1732993998

All that is left is to wish you well in your future betting as a Contented Bettor.

Happy punting!

John

Printed in Great Britain
by Amazon

16835780R00047